if you give a MOUSE a toque

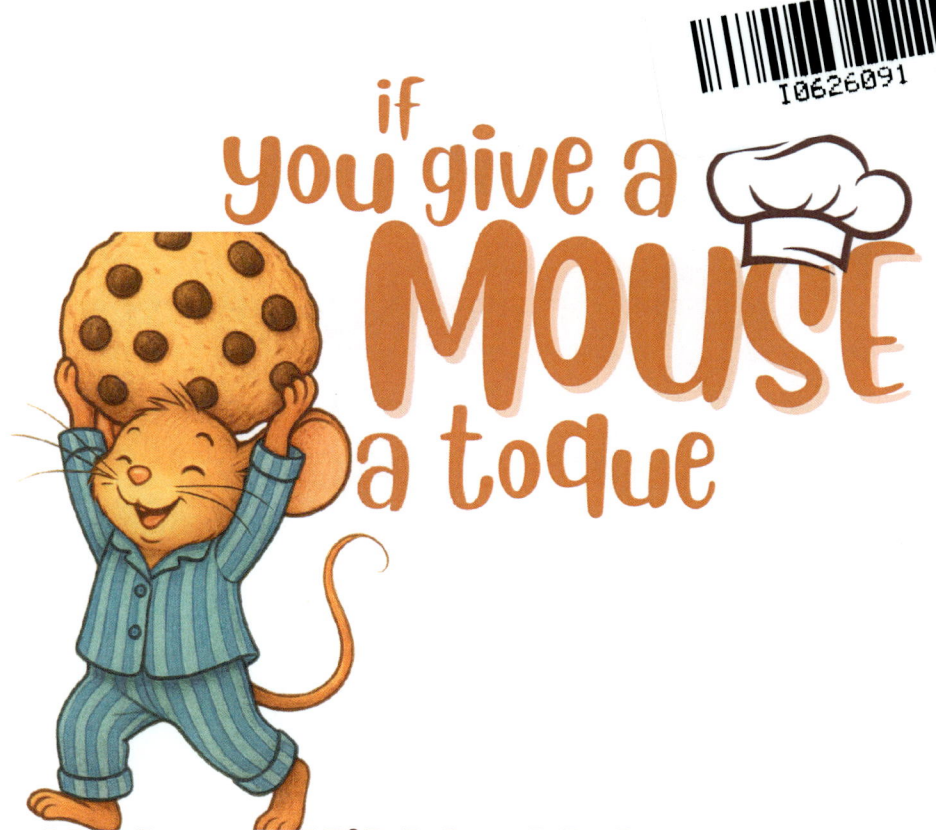

Ned and Nibbles Make

Auntie Bonnie's Chocolate Cookies

Ned and Nibbles Make Auntie Bonnie's Chocolate Cookies
© 2025 Kimm Reid

ISBN#: 978-1-998532-71-7

Published by Ahelia Publishing, LLC
Published and Printed in
United States of America

Augusta, Montana 59410

Ahelia
Publishing, LLC

KIMM REID

Ned and Nibbles Make

Auntie Bonnie's **Chocolate Cookies**

Ned woke up and stretched from one side of his teeny tiny room to the other. He had been happily dreaming about cookies... His favorite cookies... His Auntie Bonnie's CHOCOLATE CHIP COOKIES!

Ned tickled his favorite best friend, Nibbles, who was beside him stretching his own teeny tiny arms and letting out a very big yawn for such a little mouse.

"Nibbles, I was dreaming of Auntie Bonnie's cookies!" Ned said, acting like he was smelling warm cookies, fresh out of the oven.

Nibbles' whiskers twitched.

"Me too," the little brown mouse sighed.

"Let's go ask Mom if we can make Auntie Bonnie's cookies," Ned said.

He jumped out of bed and held out his hand even though he was still in his pajamas. Usually, Ned got dressed before coming out of his room, but this morning all he could think about was his auntie Bonnie's yummy chocolate chip cookies!

Nibbles, also still in his pajamas, jumped into Ned's hand and scurried up his arm, heading toward Ned's shoulder, which was where Nibbles could almost always be found.

The two friends headed out the door and down the hall, hollering for Mom.

"MOM... MOTHER... MAMMA... M-O-O-O-O-M... CAN WE MAKE AUNTIE BONNIE'S BEST CHOCOLATE CHIP COOKIES?" Ned shrieked.

They found Mom in the kitchen with her nose in the refrigerator and curlers in her hair.

"Mom, can Nibbles and I make Auntie Bonnie's chocolate chip cookies?" Ned asked his mother.

"Of course you can!" Mother answered. She began gathering the ingredients, grabbed the recipe, and set everything on the counter.

"Now, you'll need 2 sticks of butter, 1 ½ cups of white sugar and 1 cup of brown sugar, also some shortening, a few eggs, some rolled oats, some flour, some baking power and baking soda, and…"

Mom plopped down a large bag of chocolate chips, causing both Ned and Nibbles to lick their lips.

"CHOCOLATE CHIPS," they both hollered.

"Have fun," Mom said and then left the kitchen.

Ned got a big bowl from the cupboard and set it on the counter.

"OK, Nibbles. First, we need to turn on the oven." Nibbles tried to turn the dial, but it was too big, and Nibbles' hands were too small.

"Next, let's put the butter and the shortening into the bowl, and of course, the sugars." Ned scooped the sugars into cups and smoothed them off before dumping the brown sugar, and the white sugar, into the bowl.

Nibbles was so excited, he nearly fell into the bowl!

"Be careful, Nibbles," Ned laughed. "I don't want to lose you in the sugar!"

"Next, we need three eggs," Ned went to the fridge and carefully juggled three eggs. He didn't notice that Nibbles had climbed into the refrigerator, so he closed the door and went back to the cookies.

Ned cracked the eggs, one at a time, and dropped them into the mixture, stirring everything together between each egg. He started making egg jokes but when he didn't hear Nibbles laughing, Ned began to look around the kitchen.

"Nibbles... Nibbles... NIBBLES, where are you?"

Ned looked in the sugar jar. "Nibbles, are you in here? Nope! Hm. Now where did you go?" As Ned looked around puzzled, he suddenly heard a tiny, *tap, tap, tap*, coming from inside the refrigerator.

Ned opened the door, and there, with little icicles hanging from his whiskers, was Nibbles.

"Nibbles! What are you doing in there, silly little mouse?" Ned chuckled, lifted Nibbles from the refrigerator, and set him back on the counter.

"OK, now pay attention," Ned giggled. "Let's get another bowl and measure all the dry stuff into it," Ned instructed.

He grabbed a big yellow bowl from the cupboard and scooped in precisely 2 cups of rolled oats, 3 cups of flour, 2 teaspoons of baking soda and 2 teaspoons of baking powder.

Nibbles tried to pick up the big wooden spoon, but it was too heavy. Instead, Ned grabbed it, but Nibbles hung on tight.

He wanted to help Ned stir up all the ingredients!

"Now, this is the fun part, Nibbles!" Ned said. "We have to dump—carefully—this yellow bowl of dry things into the other bowl of wet things.

"Hang on, Nibbles!" Ned said. "Don't fall into the bowl! You don't want to go swimming in the cookie dough!"

Nibbles hung on to the spoon but got tired, slid down, and jumped to the side of the bowl. He sat on the side as Ned stirred and stirred and stirred some more.

Once or twice, a glob of the dough would fly up, and Nibbles would reach out and grab it, secretly licking it off his little mouse fingers.

"Now for the best ingredient of all!" Ned squealed, carefully opened the bag of chocolate chips, and with Nibbles helping him, together they poured the entire bag into the bowl.

Some of the chocolatey chocolate chips fell on the counter, and Nibbles jumped down from the bowl to retrieve the big mound of sweet chocolate.

He meant to put it in the bowl, but his paws got all chocolatey. So instead, he sat down and began to nibble on the chip.

"Oh, Nibbles. That's supposed to go into the mixture! Silly mouse," Ned laughed.

Ned skipped over to the pantry, pulled out two cookie sheets, and set them on the counter.

"Now, Nibbles," he said, "we drop big blobs onto these cookie sheets and pop them into the oven."

Very carefully, Ned scooped up balls of the cookie mixture and dropped them one by one onto the sheets.

He took a little for himself occasionally between drops, making sure to "accidentally" drop small bits onto the counter for Nibbles.

"Oops," Ned laughed. "I guess that bit's for you, Nibbles!" he'd say.

When it was time to pop the cookies into the hot oven, Ned called his mom. "MOTHER..." he shouted.

"MOM... " Nibbles echoed in his squeaky, cute little mouse voice.

Mom came into the kitchen. "Ready for the oven?" she asked.

"Yes, ma'am. I can't wait!" Ned said, his mouth beginning to water. He gave Nibbles one spoon to lick the leftover dough and began licking the other spoon himself.

"Ok, in they go!" Mom said, carefully sliding the cookie sheets into the oven.

As soon as Mom closed the oven door and set the timer for exactly nine minutes, Ned plopped himself down onto the floor, peeking into the oven and watching the cookies bake.

Nibbles stood on Ned's shoulder so he could see the cookies as well. They waited and waited, counting down the time until the timer buzzed.

It took forever for those cookies to bake.

"I can't even wait!" Ned said.

"I'm going to eat two!" Nibbles squealed.

Pretty soon, the timer buzzed, calling Mom back to the kitchen.

Mom put on her favorite red oven mitts, scooted Ned and Nibbles back from the oven so they wouldn't get burned, pulled out the cookie sheets, and set them on the counter.

"Now, you have to let them cool for five minutes," Mom said.

She set the timer again for five minutes.

"Promise?" Mom asked.

"We promise, Mom," Ned replied.

The two very impatient bakers waited and waited and waited for the timer to tick down. They played eye-spy, they did a little dance, they even counted to ten just to make the time go faster. It did not work.

"C'mon," Nibbles squeaked.

"Hurry up," Ned pleaded.

While waiting, Ned got a big glass and a small saucer from the cupboard. He poured a lot of milk in the glass, and a little milk into the saucer.

It was supposed to be to dunk the cookies in but while they were waiting for the cookies, they drank all the milk and had to get some more!

Finally, the timer buzzed, and Ned knew the cookies were ready to eat.

Ned and Nibbles jumped up and down.

"Yippee!" they squealed. Ned grabbed two big cookies and broke off a piece for Nibbles.

The two, still in their pajamas, sat on the floor, happy as could be, and enjoyed their warm cookies and cold milk.

"Mmmmm," Ned said.

"Mmmmm," Nibbles said.

"Tomorrow, let's make pancakes!"

Auntie Bonnie's
Best Chocolate Chip Cookies

Ingredients:

- 2 sticks (1 cup) softened butter
- 1 cup shortening (solid)
- 1 ½ cups white sugar
- 1 cup brown sugar
- 3 eggs
- 2 cups rolled oats
- 3 cups all purpose flour
- 2 teaspoons baking soda
- 2 teaspoons baking powder
- 1 package of chocolate chips

Instructions:

- <u>Preheat the Oven:</u>

Preheat your oven to 350 F and line baking sheets with parchment paper or silicone baking mats.

- <u>Cream Butter and Sugars:</u>

In a large bowl, use a mixer to beat the softened butter, shortening, white sugar and brown sugar together until light and fluffy. (2-3 minutes)

- <u>Add Eggs:</u>

Add eggs, one at a time and beat for 1 minute.

- <u>Mix Dry Ingredients:</u>

In a separate bowl, whisk together the rolled oats, flour, soda and baking powder.

- <u>Add Dry Ingredients to Sugar Mixture:</u>
Carefully add, a little at a time, the dry ingredients into the bowl of butter and sugars mixture. Mix well.

- <u>Add Chocolate Chips:</u>
Fold in the bag of chocolate chips with a spatula or wooden spoon.

- <u>Scoop and Shape:</u>
Use a cookie scoop or spoon to drop rounded tablespoons of dough onto prepared baking sheets, spacing them 2 inches apart.

- <u>Bake:</u>
Bake for exactly 9 minutes. Do not over bake!

- <u>Cool:</u>
Let cookies cool on baking sheets for 3-4 minutes.

Tips for making the Best Cookies even Better:

- For chewier cookies, chill the dough for 30 minutes before baking.

- Add one bag of Skor pieces to the dough.

- Sprinkle a pinch of flaky sea salt on top before baking for an extra flavour boost!

Enjoy your warm, gooey, chocolate chip cookies!

Thank you, Auntie Bonnie!

www.ingramcontent.com/pod-product-compliance
Lightning Source LLC
Chambersburg PA
CBRC090834120626
46547CB00009B/678